Bartók

THE GREAT COMPOSERS

BARTÓK

by
EVERETT HELM

FABER AND FABER
3 Queen Square
London

First published in 1971
by Faber and Faber Limited
3 Queen Square London WC1
Printed in Great Britain by
Latimer Trend & Co Ltd Plymouth

ISBN 0 571 09105 9

5660575633

Contents

Illustrations

Illustrations

LINE DRAWINGS

Music Examples

Acknowledgements

I wish to express my thanks to the following, who have kindly allowed me to reproduce copyright material: to Boosey & Hawkes Music Publishers for 'Lament' from *Twenty Hungarian Folksongs, For Children, Nos. 22, 41, Mikrokosmos No. 100*, extract from *String Quartet No. 6*; to Universal Edition (London) Ltd.; for *Rumanian Christmas Carols* Nos. 4, 5, 'Harvest Song' from *44 Duos for Two Violins*, extract from *Music for Strings, Percussion and Celesta*.

I

Childhood

Bartók's birthplace has literally disappeared from the map. When he was born in Nagyszentmiklós in 1881, this small provincial town belonged to Hungary, which was then part of the mighty Austro-Hungarian Empire. After the First World War, Hungary lost much of its former territory and was reduced to a small land. Today Bartók's home town is part of Rumania, and is called Sannicolaul-Mare. There were several nationalities living in and around Nagyszentmiklós when Bartók was a child, and he heard a variety of languages spoken: Hungarian, Rumanian and German. Later on, he learned Slovakian, French, Italian and English as well.

Nagyszentmiklós was never an important town. Situated in a fertile farming country, it was a railway junction of some local importance and a shopping centre for farmers. Its chief claim to fame, however, was its agricultural college, of which Bartók's father was the director.

Not a great deal is known about his father, whose name was also Béla. Young Béla was only seven years old when his father died. Apparently he was a strong personality, who spoke little and who ruled the household with an iron hand. His intelligence was above average, and he had a feeling for the better things of life, most of which were entirely lacking in Nagyszentmiklós. Bartók himself, the severest of critics, testified that his father was an amateur musician of considerable ability. He played several instruments, principally the cello, and even composed light music: salon pieces, dances and the like. The Bartóks' house was a centre of musical activity.

We can imagine how it fascinated the boy Béla to watch and listen from a secluded corner while his father played chamber music with his friends.

Bartók's mother, whose maiden name was Paula Voit, was an extra-ordinary woman. She came from Pressburg (in Hungarian, Pozsony), the ancient city on the Danube, quite close to Vienna, and she spoke German better than Hungarian. Without her understanding and self-sacrifice, Bartók could not possibly have become what he did. He and his mother were very close throughout her long life.

Bartók's childhood was anything but a normal and happy one. For one thing, his health was very poor. When he was three months old, he was vaccinated against smallpox and reacted 'allergically'. For the next five years, he was plagued by frightful eczema which caused him not only physical but also mental pain. It was not only the constant itching; when visitors came, the child was locked in his room because of his appearance. When he was old enough to know why, he avoided contact with strangers of his own accord. A bad case of pneumonia and a long siege of bronchitis added to the child's poor health.

From the very start Béla was alone, lonely and set apart from the others. He had few playmates and was too frail to take part in games. He spent his days at home with his mother and his younger sister Elza. Throughout his entire life his health was to give him trouble.

In early childhood Béla found pleasure and comfort in music. When he was three, his parents gave him a drum, and he loved to accompany his mother when she played the piano. At the age of four, Béla could play over forty folk-songs on the piano with one finger, and soon after that, his mother, who was a good pianist, began to give him regular lessons. Béla was seven before he started going to school because of poor health, but it was clear from the start that he was extremely intelligent and gifted. He was a willing and diligent scholar, always near the top of his class.

The death of Bartók's father put the family in a difficult situation. For some reason or other, his widow received no pension whatsoever, and she was confronted with the problem of maintaining herself and her two children single-handed. She went back to the profession for which she had been trained and took a job as schoolmistress in Nagyszőllős, a small town in North Hungary (now in the Soviet Union).

Nagyszőllős was no less provincial than Nagyszentmiklós. The music young Bartók heard there was mainly light: Hungarian imitations of Viennese dances and salon music, and so-called 'Gypsy' music, which Bartók was later to unmask as fake folk music. But there were also occasional performances of the classics such as Beethoven, Schubert, Schumann, Chopin and these made a great impression on the boy. The local organist and choirmaster, Christian Altdörfer, took a special interest in Béla and prophesied a brilliant future for him. His mother, too, realized that she had a highly-gifted son. Just to be sure, she took young Béla to Budapest and spoke with leading musicians there. Béla could have entered the Budapest

Conservatory at once, but his mother very wisely decided that he should finish his regular studies and acquire a broad, humanistic education before specializing in music.

At the age of eight, Bartók wrote his first extensive composition; he had already composed waltzes and other short dances. *The Course of the Danube* has a patriotic programme; in several short movements it describes the River Danube as it flows from its source to its mouth in the Black Sea. Some of Bartók's subtitles read: 'the Danube is happy because it is coming to Hungary ... it arrives in Budapest. Csardas ... it is sad because it is leaving Hungary ...' The mood of the music changes accordingly. In 1892, Bartók made his first public appearance as pianist in a charity concert in Nagy-szőllős, playing this naïve piece and a movement from Beethoven's Wald-stein Sonata. The eleven-year-old was a huge success.

Béla's mother had no doubt that her son was extremely gifted and she wanted him to have every advantage she could give him, considering the family's circumstances. The first eleven years of his life Béla had spent in villages with no cultural life to stimulate him. His mother made a bold decision: she took the family to Pressburg, now called Bratislava, the capital of Slovakia. Paula Voit hoped to find a teaching position there, but she was disappointed. So after a few months the family had to return to the provinces, this time to Bistritz, a small town in the eastern part of what was then Hungary and today is part of Rumania. The region, called Siebenbürgen in German and Transylvania in English, is on the fringe of the Carpathian Mountains and very beautiful. The population was even then predominantly Rumanian, but the Hungarians did everything they could to suppress the Rumanian language and culture and to 'Magyarise' the Rumanians, as well as the German minority, who had lived there for centuries.

Young Bartók fell in love with this part of the world, and he never forgot it. Years later, when he was thinking of leaving Hungary, he considered settling in Transylvania and wrote to a friend: 'Of all the parts of what was formerly Hungary, I loved this one the most.' Before the First World War, he returned often to that region to collect hundreds of Rumanian folksongs. Only now, fifty years later, have most of them been published in three thick volumes.

The Bartóks stayed only eight months in Bistritz. Musically, Béla learned very little, for he was already a better musician than anyone else in the town. But he made friends with a forester named Schönherr, also a good amateur violinist. Together they played the violin sonatas and concertos of Beethoven, whom Bartók admired above all other composers to the end of his days.

At last Bartók's mother succeeded in getting an appointment to teach in a school at Pressburg, so in 1894 the family moved there from Bistritz. Although Béla had missed most of the school year, he was allowed to take the examinations, and passed them brilliantly—so well that he was awarded a prize of fifteen florins. A classmate of Béla's has left his impression of the young scholar: 'We all knew him. His appearance was very frail (almost fragile). What distinguished him from his schoolmates and made him unforgettable were his eyes. They blazed with a mystical, fanatical flame, like the rays of his extraordinary talent and genius.'

Years later, in his short autobiography published in the magazine *Der Anbruch*, Bartók wrote about his years in Pressburg:

At that time, Pressburg had the most active musical life of any provincial city in Hungary. On the one hand I could study piano and harmony with László Erkel until I was fifteen; on the other, I could attend many orchestral and opera performances. There was also plenty of opportunity to play chamber music, and so by my eighteenth birthday I was quite well acquainted with the literature of music from Bach to Brahms and Wagner (but only up to *Tannhäuser*). At the same time I composed diligently under the strong influence of Brahms and Dohnányi.

In these few sentences, Bartók mentions two musicians who played an important part in his life. László Erkel was the son of Ferenc Erkel, Hungary's first composer of international stature. Although Ferenc Erkel's music has been almost forgotten outside of Hungary, it is important in the musical history of that country. It mainly follows Italian models, but at times it has a certain Hungarian flavour and represents one of the first attempts to produce a typically national music in Hungary. László Erkel was an excellent teacher for young Bartók, both in piano and in musical theory. Besides, he had close contact with the professional world of music, of which the country boy Béla had no conception.

Ernö Dohnányi, or Ernst von Dohnányi, as he later called himself, also played an important part in Bartók's early years. He was only four years older than Bartók but had already begun a brilliant career as pianist and composer. The two young men became close friends, despite fundamental differences in temperament, and Bartók spent many evenings in the respectable Dohnányi home, playing chamber music or talking with the famous artists who stayed with the Dohnányis when they came to Pressburg.

Dohnányi was a conservative by nature. He started out as a neo-romantic, being strongly influenced by Brahms's music; and that is more or less where he finished. His music is very well written but adds nothing new to the history of music. Soon Bartók was to be writing more modern music than Dohnányi, but, during the Pressburg years, Bartók was able to learn much from his friend.

Bartók was eighteen years old when he finished his studies in Pressburg. He had acquired a good education and had made remarkable progress in music. He knew the classical literature: Bach, Beethoven, Schubert, Chopin, Liszt, Brahms, very well indeed, but had had no contact with music that was then modern, such as that of Richard Strauss and Debussy. Such 'radical' composers were not performed in Pressburg—and very seldom even in Budapest. Bartók himself destroyed most of the music he wrote in Pressburg. The few pieces that have survived display good technical ability but little originality and are the work of a talented student who has not yet found his personal style.

Bartók's conservative early training proved to be an advantage, for his study of the great works of the classical and romantic periods provided him with standards of excellence against which he could measure his own compositions. He respected and never disregarded the great music of the past, even when he wrote his most modern and radical works. That Bartók never broke with tradition, as other composers of the twentieth century have done, is to some extent the result of his early training.

In provincial Pressburg, there was nothing more that young Bartók could learn. The next big question was where he should go to continue his studies. His first thought was Vienna, the city which attracted musicians from all over the world. He visited Vienna, played for the professors of the Conservatory and was offered a scholarship there—a great honour, considering that Bartók was a Hungarian. Probably the scholarship was for his piano playing rather than composition, for Bartók was already a brilliant pianist. After some hesitation, however, he decided on Budapest.

II

Student and Patriot

Bartók's student years at the Budapest Academy of Music were fruitful and happy. In better health than in most periods of his life, his letters reveal his good spirits. For the young man from the provinces, Budapest was very stimulating, especially compared with Pressburg. No doubt the musical life of the city was fairly traditional; but Bartók had a chance to go to the opera and to attend concerts frequently—and to broaden his horizon in many other ways as well. He had an enquiring mind and unusual powers of assimilation as well as discrimination. From all the experiences and 'discoveries' of this period, Bartók took what he could use and rejected what did not suit his temperament. He became acquainted with the standard operatic repertoire, which to him had no great appeal. Even then, as later in life, his main interest was in orchestral concerts and chamber music. His critical powers also developed rapidly. In a letter to his mother he wrote about a recital by the famous pianist Emil Sauer: 'It is interesting the way he poses. He lifts his hands a metre in the air, he shakes his head about, he raises his eyes to heaven, then he meditates before each number; and then, as if he suddenly remembered what piece he was going to play, he begins, etc. (Perhaps the ladies like this sort of thing.)'

An interesting criticism from a nineteen-year-old, who all his life was set against any kind of pretence and who never put on any kind of show.

During his student days, Bartók led a much more active social life than at any later period. He went to parties and played often in the salons of various musical personages. He was well known as a brilliant pianist rather than as a composer.

As a matter of fact, he was quite unhappy with his composition teacher, János Koessler, a conservative and rather pedantic person who had studied with Brahms. Later on, Bartók recognized the better side of Koessler, but at this time he wrote: 'Today I showed Koessler my slow movement. He said: "A slow movement must express love; there is no hint of love in

Bartók's parents, Béla and Paula Bartók

Left, the composer aged ten with his sister, Elza; *below*, Bartók with his mother and sister during a summer holiday in about 1900

yours . . ." Koessler always says "To write an Adagio one must have had certain experiences." Well, I don't think that experiences have so much influence on the quality of a composition.'

The performance of a new and very modern orchestral piece suddenly changed everything. In his autobiographical sketch, Bartók wrote: 'The first performance in Budapest of *Also sprach Zarathustra*, in 1902, tore me like a stroke of lightning out of this stagnation. The work filled most of the local musicians with horror, but I was most enthusiastic. At last I could see a new direction. I plunged into the study of Strauss's scores and began to compose again.'

New music began to pour from Bartók's pen. Between 1902 and 1903 he wrote a symphony, his first and last of which the manuscript has been lost, a Scherzo for Orchestra, a Sonata for Violin and Piano, eight songs, four piano pieces and the symphonic poem *Kossuth*. None of these works is of great importance and none gives a hint of the later Bartók. It is well-written music showing the influence of Brahms and Richard Strauss but without the originality of his later works.

When Bartók received his diploma from the Budapest Academy of Music in 1903, nobody could have prophesied that he would become one of the great composers of the twentieth century. Many predicted, however, that he would have a successful career as a concert pianist.

After graduation, Bartók spent the summer in Gmunden, Upper Austria, working with Dohnányi and orchestrating *Kossuth*. In November 1904, he played Beethoven's Fifth Piano Concerto at the Vienna Konzertverein, and in December he gave a solo recital in Berlin, for which he received good but by no means rave notices. More important, Ferruccio Busoni, the great piano virtuoso, composer and aesthetician, attended the recital and was impressed. Busoni was among the first to sense Bartók's genius. Later he was to help with encouragement and advice.

At the beginning of 1904, Bartók suddenly became a celebrity, at least in his own country. The premier of his symphonic poem *Kossuth* was his first success as a composer and the only one he was to have for years to come.

Actually, the success of *Kossuth* was more political than musical. The young, inexperienced Bartók was caught up in the wave of patriotism that swept Hungary at that time. His patriotic feelings did not last long, but they were intensely felt. Bartók appeared in public in native peasant costume, and made his sister do the same when a piece of his was performed. In his letters he attacked the Austrians for their repression of 'Hungarianism'. He used stationery imprinted with the Hungarian coat of arms, the first line of the Hungarian national anthem and the motto: 'God bless Hungary.' On some letters he added, in his own hand, 'and save it from the Habsburg family'. He berated his mother, who had been brought up to speak German, for not writing and speaking Hungarian.

In this frame of mind, Bartók composed *Kossuth*. The symphonic poem for orchestra consists of ten fairly short movements, glorifying the national hero Lajos Kossuth, who led the Hungarian Revolution of 1848 and was president of the republic during the four months of its existence. Musically, *Kossuth* is probably the worst piece Bartók ever wrote. It is full of sound and fury, bombastic, banal, derivative and vulgar in its programmatic picture-painting.

But for once in his life, Bartók was the right man with the right work at the right moment. The Hungarians loved *Kossuth* because of its political implications. An incident at one of the rehearsals was taken up by the newspapers and added to Bartók's notoriety. In a number of passages he parodied the Austrian national anthem, making it sound grotesque, and the Austrian trumpeter refused to play these passages. When the piece was performed in Budapest it had a great success, and Bartók was given an ovation.

The following year, *Kossuth* was performed in Manchester by the Hallé Orchestra under Hans Richter. Quite naturally, it got bad reviews; the British critics and audience were not carried away by the politics involved. The critic of the *Guardian* pointed out the many passages that were practically cribbed from Richard Strauss (especially from *Ein Heldenleben*); he recognized Bartók's technical ability and hoped that the young Hungarian would soon get over his Strauss craze. A solo recital which Bartók gave two days after the concert got only moderate praise. It cannot be said that his first visit to England was very successful.

Bartók did get over his Strauss craze fairly soon. And he soon realized that the narrow kind of patriotism of his brief *Kossuth* period was a mistake. He became a citizen of the world without becoming any the less a Hungarian.

III

An Eventful Year

The year 1905 was one of the most important in Bartók's life. In twelve months' time he suffered a great disappointment, made an important discovery, experienced a great revelation and arrived at an important conclusion. The disappointment was his failure to win a place in the Rubinstein Competition in Paris. The discovery was the city of Paris and all that goes with it. The revelation came from his first contact with genuine Hungarian folk music. And the conclusion was to do with the music of Franz Liszt and its place in the history of music.

Bartók went to Paris to take part as pianist and composer in the international Rubinstein Competition. He wrote to his mother about the outcome: 'Unfortunately I had no success. That I didn't win the piano prize is not surprising and doesn't depress me, but the way in which the prize for composition was handled is absolutely shocking. The piano prize went to Backhaus. . . . In composition, there were only five contestants.'

The jury decided not to give the first or second prize. Honorable mentions were awarded to a certain Brugnoli and to Bartók. The outraged Bartók sent his diploma back. He wrote to his mother: 'Brugnoli's works were nothing but worthless compilations. It is scandalous that the jury didn't see how much better my pieces are.'

This was not to be the last time Bartók took offence when he had been unjustly neglected. It was neither wounded pride nor arrogance; rather, the sure knowledge of his own worth. The Piano Concerto which failed to win the prize has been lost—or perhaps Bartók himself destroyed it. It seems likely, however, that the Scherzo for Piano and Orchestra was one of this concerto's movements. Although it has no comparison with Bartók's mature works, it is a very good piece indeed, considering that it was written by a twenty-three-year-old.

However irritated he was by the outcome of the competition, Bartók did not let this spoil his visit. He went everywhere and saw everything in Paris,

19

like the most avid tourist, and loved every minute of it. He even went one evening to the Moulin Rouge, but spent most of his time in the museums, churches and other famous buildings of 'the city of light'. The first visit to Paris is a great event in anyone's life and certainly was for the sensitive Bartók, whose ability to absorb and digest new experiences was prodigious.

We are lucky to have several letters which Bartók wrote from Paris. Some of them, addressed to Irmy Jurkovics, a young lady from Nagyszent-miklós, are a strange mixture of philosophy, aesthetics and juvenile chatter.

A drawing from one of Bartók's letters dated September 1906

One letter to his mother is extremely interesting and revealing. After describing his association with Cubans, Dutch, Americans, Germans, Spaniards and Turks, Bartók says that suddenly he feels very much alone. 'And I prophesy that this spiritual loneliness will be my fate. Although I search for an ideal companion, I know that I do so in vain. If I should some day find someone, disappointment would be bound to follow after a short time. . . .' His prophecy of loneliness was unfortunately true. Throughout his life he was alone, even when surrounded by many people.

It was in 1905 that Bartók had his first contact with real Hungarian folk music, and it came as a revelation. It is strange that this music had not been discovered years earlier, for it had always been there, sung by the peasants in the villages of the remote parts of Hungary, with a tradition going back for many centuries. The contact came about through another young Hungarian musician, Zóltan Kodály, who had discovered genuine Hungarian folk music and shared his discovery with Bartók. Both of them were astonished and fascinated by its natural appeal. Compared to the more

Rumanian Folksong: No. 5, from *Seven Sketches for Piano*

In Walachian Style: No. 6, from *Seven Sketches for Piano*

sophisticated music of the gypsies, it is plain, like the people who have passed it on from father to son, mother to daughter, for generations. But it is genuine and honest; its simplicity conveys deep emotion and elemental feelings that have not been weakened by the refinements of 'civilisation'.

The purely musical side was also a revelation to Bartók. Much of the music is modal, that is to say, it employs scales that were once in common use but that were gradually replaced by major and minor. Like many other composers of the twentieth century, Bartók felt a need to find new forms of melody and harmony. Some, like Schoenberg, turned their backs entirely on tonality and developed atonal and twelve-tone music. Others, like Bartók and Stravinsky, kept the *principle* of tonality but expanded it by the free use of dissonance, by new relationships between harmonies, etc. To put it plainly: Bartók continued to employ tonality in a general sort of way, but he broke all the rules of traditional harmonic practice.

Simply breaking rules is of course not enough; you need something to take the place of what you have rejected. And this is where folk music came to Bartók's aid. He did not *imitate* peasant music, nor use it as a kind of decoration, nor as something exotic, as many composers have done. He first digested the folk music completely and then used it as part of his personal idiom.

In 1905 Bartók came to the conclusion that the music of Franz Liszt was misunderstood by most people, including himself. It is true that Liszt wrote a good deal of salon music of a virtuoso nature. But in many works he showed originality. Studying the less popular works of Liszt, Bartók realised 'the true importance of this artist; I felt that he was more original than Wagner or Strauss'. From now on, the music and the example of Liszt were to play an important part in Bartók's creative thought.

IV

The Young Professor

Bartók now had three major interests: composition, folk music and his career as pianist. During the next few years, roughly until 1912, he worked hard at all three. Considering his frail constitution, it is difficult to imagine how he was able to accomplish all that he did. He lived for his work and in it found his greatest satisfaction. He had been a serious boy, and he became a serious young man who had little time for amusements or relaxation.

In 1906 Béla made a long concert tour as accompanist of the child prodigy violinist Ferenc Vecsey. Together they played many concerts in Spain and Portugal. This concert tour opened Bartók's eyes to the problems and disadvantages of a career as virtuoso. He wrote to his mother: 'This kind of forced labour is dreadful. Because of all the practising he has to do, young Vecsey sees almost nothing of the world.' Bartók probably realized at that time how much a virtuoso has to give up for a successful career. He was certainly interested in too many other things to be able to concentrate exclusively on playing the piano. If he had done so, he might well have been one of the most famous pianists of his time. But he would probably never have been a great composer.

As it was, Bartók became a great teacher of piano. In 1907 he was appointed Professor of Piano at the Budapest Academy of Music, succeeding his own former teacher István Thomán. For so young a person, this appointment was a great honour, and it provided Bartók with a steady salary for many years. He kept the position until 1934. He did not always enjoy teaching, but he fulfilled his duties at the Academy very conscientiously.

One of the advantages of Bartók's teaching position was that he had a good deal of free time for his own work. In the summer holidays, he put his knapsack on his back and went into the Hungarian hinterland to collect peasant music. In June of 1908 he attended the master classes given by Ferruccio Busoni at Baden, near Vienna. When Bartók played his fourteen *Bagatelles*, Busoni remarked: 'something really new at last'.

24

The cover design for Bartók's Ten Easy Pieces composed in 1908

Ten Easy Pieces: No. 5

The Young Professor

It is amazing how Bartók had progressed during the five years since *Kossuth* and had begun to write music that revealed his own musical personality. His interest in peasant music accounts for this change to some extent. But in these early works another influence is noticeable: that of the great French composer Claude Debussy. It was Bartók's first encounter with the modern music of his time, and it made a great impression. The First Violin Concerto and the *Two Portraits for Orchestra*, the First String Quartet and the opera *Bluebeard's Castle* show Bartók's familiarity with the works of Debussy, as do many short piano pieces composed at this time.

V

Disappointments

Thanks to Busoni, Bartók was invited to conduct a movement of his Second Suite for Orchestra and to play the solo part of his Scherzo for Piano and Orchestra at a concert in the Beethoven Hall in Berlin. It was the first and last time Bartók ever conducted an orchestra. The Berlin press was not friendly towards this 'modern' music, which seems so unexceptional to us today.

Busoni also wrote a letter to the great publishing firm of Breitkopf and Härtel, recommending Bartók's *Bagatelles*. The publishers sent back the manuscript with the usual polite excuses. Together with other early works, the *Bagatelles* were published in Budapest.

With letters of recommendation from Busoni in his pocket, Bartók went again to Paris; it was his last attempt to make 'important connections'. Bartók describes the results in a letter to his mother: 'D'Indy rejected me completely: "Il faut choisir les thèmes . . ." that sums up his opinion. This meeting with d'Indy was like a famous professor graciously receiving a pupil, a beginner, to whom he gives instructions. Well, I've had enough of that, thank you, and I don't need any more.'

The story of Bartók's meeting with Isidore Philipp, a pianist and teacher of Hungarian origin, is probably true. The French pianist asked Bartók whom he would like to meet in Paris, and Bartók said he wanted to meet Debussy. 'But Debussy is a boor . . . do you want to be insulted by Debussy?' asked Philipp. To which Bartók replied 'Yes!' Unfortunately the meeting did not take place.

Bartók was disgusted with the whole affair. He realised clearly that he was no good at musical diplomacy. He could not flatter, he could not hide his true feelings and opinions, and he could not ask for favours. In short, he could not 'operate' in order to get ahead. Having realized this, he withdrew even more into himself and built up a protective shell of pride and reticence, hoping that he would gain recognition—and performances—on the sheer merits of his music.

28

14 Bagatelles for Piano: No. 2

Allegro giocoso (♩ = 76)

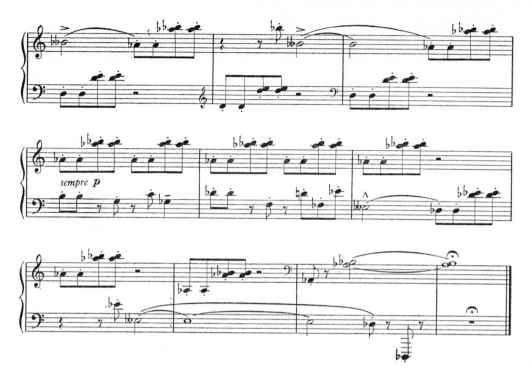

Recognition, however, was slow in coming. Especially in his own country he met with strong opposition. The conservative Budapest audiences and press were hostile to innovations of any kind. As early as 1907, Bartók wrote: 'I shall no longer bother with the Hungarian oxen—that is the Hungarian public. Kodály says quite rightly: "pheasant is not for donkeys; if we feed them with it, they become ill". So let's leave the donkeys in peace and take our serious work abroad.'

Bartók especially resented being told repeatedly to return to his early style. In 1905 a critic had praised him as a 'master of salon music'. But in 1907 the leading newspaper *Pesti Naplo* called his Second Suite for Orchestra 'a wretched contrived miscarriage—it can only make one angry and sorry that a man of such undoubted genius can become the victim of artistic caprices and aberrations that ruin his talent'.

We cannot imagine today that Bartók's First String Quartet, 1908, could receive a review like the one which appeared in the Budapest German newspaper *Pester Lloyd*: 'This is an astounding mixture of strange thoughts, genuine and deep feeling and empty, fragmentary music—tortured and repulsive.' This First Quartet is a splendid piece, which sounds as fresh today as when it was written. The string quartet is perhaps the most difficult form of composition; its intimate character means that the composer cannot rely on any of the effects a big symphony orchestra can produce. Quite rightly, Bartók's six-string quartets are regarded as the very heart of his work. They are not always easy to listen to, but with repeated hearings they give us the clue to Bartók's development and to his spiritual message. They represent the most important contribution to the quartet form since Beethoven and are without equal in the twentieth century.

Bartók, Kodály and several other musicians were so disturbed by the backwardness of the Budapest public that they formed the New Hungarian Society for Music. Their aim was to present annual series of concerts featuring modern music of all nationalities, including, of course, Hungarian. To finance an orchestra, they needed the support of the Hungarian Ministry of Culture. When this support was refused, the project collapsed. Needless to say, this was a great disappointment for Bartók—one of a whole series of disappointments that left him in a very depressed state of mind. His career as concert pianist had made little progress; his compositions were neglected abroad and at home. To crown all, his opera *Bluebeard's Castle* was rejected by the Budapest Opera. In 1911 the City of Budapest had held a competition for the best opera, with the promise of performance for the winning work. The jury decided that none of the operas submitted was good enough to be produced. *Bluebeard* had to wait seven more years before it saw the light of day.

Besides all these professional disillusionments, Bartók's private life seems to have been anything but happy during these years. We have very little to go on, and Bartók never discussed his private affairs with anyone. But from some letters, and from the testimony of those who knew him at that period, we know that between 1906 and 1911 he went through an emotional crisis. When he was twenty-six, Bartók fell in love with the twenty-year-old violinist Stefi Geyer. It was a strange love affair that lasted less than two years. In many of his compositions written in 1907 and 1908, Bartók includes Stefi's 'Leitmotiv' or leading motive. We find it, for instance, in the First Violin Concerto which Bartók dedicated to Stefi and which was considered lost for over fifty years.

The few published letters from Bartók to Stefi Geyer show rather plainly why the match did not last. He upbraids Stefi for not thinking as he did and accuses her of being a moral coward because she has no interest in the books he tells her to read. In their preaching and superior tone, these are very curious love letters indeed.

It is not surprising that Bartók was never 'lucky in love' since he made such high demands. He expected such perfection and such mental obedience in his ideal woman as is not to be found among mortals.

Disappointments

Without telling anyone, Bartók suddenly married his pupil, Márta Ziegler, who was then (in 1909) sixteen years old. He broke the news to his mother during their evening meal by saying: 'Márta will stay here. She is my wife.'

Apparently the marriage was not a very happy one and it would be hard to say whose fault it was. One can only feel sorry for Márta, who certainly meant well and did her best. But it is not easy to live with a genius—and especially with one who is subject to chronic periods of deep depression. After fourteen years, the marriage ended in divorce. It must be added that however difficult he was at times, Bartók always conducted himself with the greatest integrity. On this point there is complete agreement.

Everything combined to put Bartók in a depressed, pessimistic frame of mind: his professional failures, his personal disappointments and his recurring poor health. In 1912 he practically broke off contact with the world and retired for nine years into a sort of self-imposed inner exile. To a friend he wrote: 'I have resigned myself to writing only for my desk drawer from now on. As far as appearances abroad are concerned, I have tried vainly for eight years to get somewhere. I'm tired of it and have made no more efforts for a year. If anybody wants to perform something of mine he can buy the published works; they can be performed without me.'

During his first years of inner exile Bartók composed very little music. In the summer of 1912 he travelled with his wife to Norway. In 1913 he went alone to North Africa to collect Arab folk music, and in the summer of 1914, he made a vacation trip to France. No sooner had he returned to Budapest than the First World War broke out and added to his dejected frame of mind. Now he could not even travel, and worst of all, he could not go on his expeditions to collect folk music.

It was his interest in folk music, however, that kept him going during these dark years and that finally helped to restore his troubled spirits. During this period, Bartók spent most of his time transcribing, studying and classifying the thousands of folk tunes he had collected on his many expeditions between 1905 and 1913. At first, he had tried to write these tunes down on the spot, but this method involved great difficulties. So he soon bought himself an Edison recording machine, which enabled him to record the peasants' music directly on wax cylinders. Turning a crank by hand, he could generate electricity by means of a magneto, and the peasants had to sing into a large horn which was part of the primitive equipment. Many of them were afraid of the machine; some thought that it would swallow up their voices and never give them back. But Bartók had a way with these simple people, and usually it didn't take long before he had completely

Bartók in Budapest, 1901

Bartók, aged twenty-three, with his sister, Elza

Recording folk-songs on a phonograph in 1908

Bartók (*seated left*) with Zoltán Kodály (*seated second from right*) and the
Waldbauer Quartet

'For Children', the cover design for the studies which Bartók composed from 1908 to 1909

For Children: No. 22

gained their confidence. These collecting expeditions were anything but comfortable, yet Bartók loved the contact with nature and the peasants. He later wrote: 'The happiest days of my life were those which I spent with the peasants in their villages.'

For his own happiness Bartók needed to believe in the simple, uncomplicated peasant and the happy peasant village. So he created this image and found consolation in it. And there is good reason to believe that much of his music is in some way connected with natural phenomena—a kind of secret tone painting inspired by nature. The violinist André Gertler describes how during a performance of the *Music for Strings, Percussion and Celesta*, Bartók whispered to him: 'Do you hear that? It is the sea.'

Folk music occupied Bartók from early youth until his death. Measured

Rumanian Christmas Carols: No. 4

Rumanian Christmas Carols: No. 5

in terms of hours, days and weeks, he spent more time on folklore than he did on composition. What began almost as a sideline became a profession. Bartók was a pioneer and an authority in the field of folk music—now called ethnomusicology. He published many books and articles on the subject, gave many lectures and was internationally recognized as a leading expert.

It is not surprising that nearly everything he composed during this period of inner exile was connected directly with folk music. In 1915 alone he wrote the Piano Sonatina (based on Rumanian folk melodies), the *Rumanian Folk Dances for Piano*, the *Rumanian Christmas Carols for Piano*, *Two Rumanian Folksongs for Women's Chorus* and *Nine Rumanian Folksongs for Voice and Piano*. He also worked on the ballet *The Wooden Prince*, which is saturated with the spirit of Hungarian folksong; and from 1916 to 1920 he composed *Eight Hungarian Folksongs for Voice and Piano*, *Three Hungarian Folksongs for Piano*,

Disappointments

Five Slovakian Folksongs for Male Chorus, Four Slovakian Folksongs for Mixed Chorus, Fifteen Hungarian Peasant Songs for Piano and *Improvisations on Hungarian Peasant Songs for Piano*.

In some of the pieces, Bartók keeps the original melody intact and adds a simple and appropriate accompaniment, in style with the tune itself. Such simple settings demand great taste and skill of a special kind. The accompaniment must not get in the way of the melody, but at the same time it must have some interest and meaning in itself. In the two short *Colinde* or *Rumanian Christmas Carols* notice how restrained the treatment is. In No. 4, the melody is heard first in the middle register of the piano, then an octave lower. The first time it is accompanied by sparse chords that contribute two 'spicy' dissonances (bars 5 and 7); the second time, the accompaniment is linear and forms an interesting counterpoint. In the fifth carol, the melody is heard three times in the same register. Only the accompaniment changes, just enough to supply plenty of variety, while the principle of unvaried repetition, typical of some folk music, is maintained in the right hand. In other pieces, the accompaniment is more involved, and the material is varied and developed to a certain extent, as in the touchingly beautiful 'Panasz' or 'Lament' from the *Twenty Hungarian Folksongs for Voice and Piano* —one of the finest song cycles of the twentieth century. The piano has a short introduction (and postlude) in which the 'snap' rhythm (♪♩..) is prominent and forms a kind of ostinato (or regularly repeated figure) throughout the short piece. When the melody returns for the second strophe, Bartók varies the accompaniment, subtly introducing more harmonic variety and adding short motives that are taken from the vocal melody: at bar 28, the piano imitates the preceding vocal phrase at the pitch of a fourth below; at bar 30, the imitation is in inversion; at bar 34 the left hand repeats the voice's motive of bar 33 a second lower; and at bar 38 the imitation is at the sixth below. It is impossible to imagine a more perfect setting of this moving melody than Bartók's—or to think of another composer who could have achieved such expressive depth with so few notes.

In a certain number of pieces the treatment of the folk material is more elaborate, and the work stands somewhere between a folksong 'setting' and a composition using folksong elements. The *Improvisations on Hungarian Peasant Songs*, opus 20, are a good example of this more complicated treatment. This piece, with its involved harmonies and virtuoso piano technique, is about as far as Bartók went in 'transforming' folk music into concert music.

37

'Lament' from *Twenty Hungarian Folksongs*

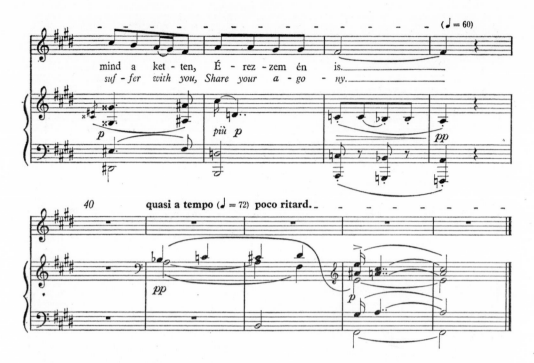

mind a ket - ten, É - rez - zem én is.
suf - fer with you, Share your a - go - ny.

The most astonishing—and effective—'manipulation' of folk music is to be found in the 44 Duos for Two Violins, which Bartók composed in 1931. Like the *Mikrokosmos*, these Duos are progressive in difficulty and are to some extent pedagogical in nature, although many are entirely suitable for concert performance. All except two are based on genuine peasant songs, and it is amazing what Bartók has done with them without detracting from their folk character. The short 'Harvest Song', for example, is bi-tonal throughout: one violin has no key signature, while the other is notated with six sharps or five flats. From bar 16 (Tempo I) to 20, the melodic material of bars 1 to 5 is heard in exact inversion. At bar 21 (Tempo II) the canon of bars 6 to 15 is now heard in 'stretto'—that is to say, the second voice enters after a quaver rest rather than after a minim rest as at bar 6. Yet despite all these contrapuntal and harmonic tricks, the music sounds fresh and spontaneous.

Bartók wrote many works in which he did not use any folk tunes at all, but which seem to be strongly influenced by folk music. This category includes some of his masterpieces: *Dance Suite, Cantata Profana, Music for Strings, Percussion and Celesta* and *Concerto for Orchestra*. One would swear that the theme of the last movement of the *Dance Suite* is a real folk tune if one didn't know that Bartók himself invented it. The tender, winsome melody

'Harvest Song' from *44 Duos for Two Violins*

of the ritornello in the *Dance Suite* is another superb example of invented folk music—unimaginable without the long years of intimate contact with the real thing.

The same is eminently true of the short piece 'Népdaféle', number 100 in the *Mikrokosmos*, that unique collection of piano pieces which Bartók worked on intermittently between 1926 and 1939. The melody is diatonic and modal (with the flat seventh degree); although it revolves around the note A, this note is not felt as a 'tonic' in the usual sense. The harmonies are even less tonal in their implications, being the result of contrapuntal voice leading in the accompanying voice (left hand). In its irregular metres and phrasing ($\frac{5}{8} + \frac{5}{8} + \frac{3}{8}$) the piece reflects the rhythmic construction of many folk melodies. After the tune has been heard in the right hand, it passes to the left hand, where it is repeated in varied form, while the accompaniment, now in the right hand, is also given a new contour. The principle of constant melodic, rhythmic and harmonic variation of 'germ' themes or motives is basic to Bartók's method of composition. The principles and techniques which we see here so clearly underly many of his greatest works.

These two activities—composition and folk music research—are really quite different in nature. But in Bartók's case they go hand in hand. If he had not spent so much time and energy collecting and studying folk music, he could not have written the kind of music he did.

'Like a Folksong' from *Mikrokosmos*: No. 100

VI

The Stage Works

Gradually, Bartók overcame the spiritual crisis that had led him in 1912 to renounce the world and retire into himself. The first step towards recovery from this depression was a commission to write a ballet for the Budapest Opera. The director of the opera was very anxious that Béla Balázs' fairytale *The Wooden Prince* should be made into a ballet, and he was even willing to accept the music of the wild modernist Bartók as part of the package deal. Spurred on by the prospect of a performance, Bartók finished the score in 1916, and *The Wooden Prince* was given its first performance in May 1917.

After years of mediocre performances by uninterested conductors, Bartók had the good fortune of having his ballet entrusted to Egisto Tango, an Italian who appeared regularly in Budapest as guest conductor. The regular conductors of the Opera had all refused to rehearse the work. Tango set about with all his energy to give the strange, unconventional score the best possible performance. He demanded and received the unheard-of number of thirty rehearsals. But things went badly from the start, much to the satisfaction of Bartók's adversaries. The orchestral players declared the music unplayable, and it seemed a foregone conclusion that the première would turn into a *scandale*.

To the astonishment of everyone, most of all the composer, the première was a towering success—the first important one of Bartók's life. Tango conducted with such skill and zeal that the orchestra forgot its intention to mutiny and they played as never before. The audience gave Bartók an ovation, and there was nothing for the habitually unfriendly press to do but join in the applause. Budapest had finally realized that Bartók was not an *enfant terrible* but a genius. A year later, due to Tango's continual efforts, *Bluebeard's Castle* was performed for the first time and with equally great success. Bartók's third stage work, *The Miraculous Mandarin*, did not fare so well. It was written in 1918 but first performed in 1926 in Cologne, where

44

it was withdrawn after one performance. It was not performed in Budapest until 1946.

There is no concrete proof that Bartók intended his three stage works to be given on a single evening. But he may well have, for they form a psychological and philosophical unity. The Budapest Opera has performed them for years to packed houses, and the impression is that the pieces do in fact belong together—despite the differences in subject matter and musical treatment. One also has the feeling that the trilogy is to some extent autobiographical, that it reflects Bartók's own spiritual progress from dark despair to the hope of salvation.

In the opera, the old fairy tale of the cruel knight is transformed into a deeply symbolical piece with strong psychological overtones. Bluebeard appears here as a tragic figure: lonely, taciturn, and enigmatic—like Bartók himself. The seven doors which Judith insists on opening lead not only to gardens, lakes of tears, and torture chambers but also into Bluebeard's very soul. At the start of the work, there appears to be some hope of a happy ending. With the opening of the fifth door, disclosing Bluebeard's endless domains, Bluebeard has grown to heroic stature, worthy of Judith's love. The music, with its broad noble chords, is exultant. But Judith proves unequal to the situation. In spite of Bluebeard's warnings and pleas, Judith demands the sixth and seventh keys, which reveal symbolically the deepest secrets of his innermost being. From this moment on the roles are reversed. Judith is no longer the loving partner but blind instinct, unworthy of Bluebeard's love. When the last door opens, Bluebeard's former wives appear, lifeless and silent: Morning, Noon and Evening. 'Of all women, Judith, you were the most beautiful,' cries Bluebeard. She, Night, follows the others through the seventh door, and Bluebeard remains alone.

Bluebeard's happiness is destroyed through Judith's (symbolizing the world's?) lack of comprehension. From beginning to end one is held spellbound by the tragedy of two human beings doomed to misunderstanding and by the intensity of the musical utterance. The work ends in despair. As Bluebeard says: 'Now it is eternal night—always, forever.'

The Wooden Prince is also the story of two lovers, but the development reverses that of *Bluebeard*. At first the Prince is thwarted in his desire to reach the Princess's tower by the machinations of the fairy. To attract the indifferent Princess's attention, the Prince decorates a stick with his cloak and crown. The Princess dances with the puppet but soon becomes bored. She notices the Prince, for the first time. But now the fairy changes sides in favour of the Prince. Only when the Princess cuts off her hair, as a symbol of self-humiliation, is the pair happily united. The deeper significance of the ballet lies in the fact that happiness is achieved not through the fairy's magic but through the Prince's steadfast devotion and the Princess's self-abasement. The overcoming of obstacles separating human beings from each other (whether as individuals or nations) was a life-long dream of the solitary, disappointed, but doggedly hopeful Bartók.

It is of more than passing interest to note how the opera and the ballet are joined musically. *Bluebeard* ends pianissimo on C sharp in the lowest register: the effect is one of utter exhaustion. *The Wooden Prince* begins pianissimo with a long bass pedal on C, over which the 'bright' tonality of C major becomes clearly evident. One has the feeling of ascending out of the slough of despair.

Bluebeard is outspokenly pessimistic; *The Wooden Prince* is optimistic; *The Miraculous Mandarin* might be described as realistic. The subject matter, involving three thugs and a prostitute, is not conventional. The score is aggressive and tough in its characterization of evil and sensuality. Yet far from being a thriller with a sensational plot, the piece is both strong social criticism and an affirmation of man's ability to conquer circumstances through courage and magnanimity.

When the girl, forced into prostitution by the thugs, feels spontaneous sympathy for the penniless and shy student, she starts her upward climb; when she overcomes her abhorrence of the fearsome mandarin and embraces him, she is redeemed. And this same symbolic gesture of compassion releases the enigmatic, lustful mandarin from his suffering.

In all three works, the theme remains 'man's struggle for spiritual salvation'. The opera ends in hopelessness; the ballet's solution is perhaps too easy. The pantomime achieves a true catharsis. It cannot be a conventional happy ending; rather, it indicates symbolically the hard, inexorable, and solitary way man must go to achieve his redemption. Bartók knew well that for him there was no other way. With stoical courage he followed it to the end of his life.

VII

Return to the World

At the beginning of the 1920s, Bartók returned to the international world of music which he had renounced in 1912. After the confusion of the post-war period—inflation, revolution and counter-revolution—the situation in Hungary became more stable. But the country had been reduced to a third of its former size, and a great deal of Bartók's activity as a pianist took him outside its borders. At home he continued to teach piano at the Academy of Music, and during the first few years of the 1920s, he spent a great deal of time preparing two important books for publication: *Folk Music of the Rumanians of Maramures* and *The Hungarian Folksong*. Both books were published in German and did much to establish Bartók as a leading authority in this field.

Between the composition of *The Miraculous Mandarin* in 1918 and the year 1926, Bartók wrote very little music. All through his life, in fact, periods of intense creative activity alternated with stretches of comparative calm. In seven years, he produced only five pieces: in 1919, none; in 1920 the *Improvisations on Hungarian Peasant Songs for Piano*; in 1921, the First and in 1922 the Second Sonata for Violin and Piano; in 1923 the *Dance Suite*; in 1924 the unimportant *Village Scenes for Voice and Piano*; in 1925, no new work.

Bartók made his first extended tour abroad in 1920, playing in England and France and visiting Germany. At his first concert in England since 1905, he performed the new First Violin Sonata with Jelly d'Aranyi, for whom he had written it. Bartók wrote to his mother: 'Yesterday I played a "private" concert in London, at the home of the Hungarian ambassador. Although it was not public, a very favourable review appeared in *The Times*. But even before this there had been announcements of my appearance in the *Daily Telegraph* and *Daily Mail*, as well as in two musical journals. I was received with great interest and kindness.'

From London Bartók went on to Paris, where he also had considerable success and made the acquaintance of leading musicians—among them Henri Prunières, editor of the important *Revue Musicale* and a weighty figure in Parisian musical life. Again Bartók wrote to his mother: 'The concert was a good success. Afterwards there was a supper, given by Prunières, at which more than half of the "world's leading composers" were present: Ravel, Stravinsky, Szymanowski and others. Most of them were very much impressed by the Violin Sonata . . .'

Bartók playing with Joseph Szigeti in 1927

On the way from Paris to Budapest, Bartók stopped in Frankfurt am Main for the first performances outside Hungary of *Bluebeard* and *The Wooden Prince*. The works had little success, but perhaps this was due to the performances, with which Bartók was not at all happy.

The year 1922 saw the first in a series of performances of Bartók's work at international music festivals; this time at Frankfurt, where his First Violin Sonata was heard. The success of this festival led to the founding of the International Society for Contemporary Music (I.S.C.M.), which still exists today and sponsors an annual festival of modern music seldom heard

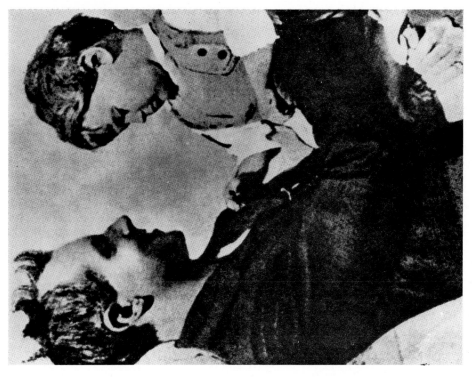

A photograph taken by Kodály of Bartók and his son
Béla jr., in 1913

The composer aged thirty-one

The composer in 1916

A drawing of Bartók giving a piano recital
in Hungary

With Joseph Szigeti who made a piano recording
with Bartók in America in 1940

in regular subscription concerts. To be sure, these I.S.C.M. festivals were, and are, fairly private affairs, attended almost exclusively by composers, musicians and press. But they provided an important 'showcase' for young radicals, including Schoenberg, Stravinsky, Milhaud, Hindemith, Honegger and many others. By their very nature, they became a 'must' for the international music press, and the composers performed became known, at least by name, to a broad public through articles and reviews.

Although Bartók's name became widely known through performances at the I.S.C.M. and other such societies, his music had scant success with the general public, for whom it was too extreme. An exception to the rule was his Dance Suite, composed for the 500th anniversary of the city of Budapest. After a highly successful première in 1923, the Dance Suite swept the musical world; in Germany alone, it had some fifty performances in a single season. It is an extraordinary work, fresh and full of invention. In it, Bartók did not for a minute write down to the audience; but he did produce a piece that is easily accessible, one that did not present the stylistic problems that are found in many of his other works. It is essentially a piece using the normal major-minor scales, melodically appealing and formally clear, in which the rhythmic factor is strong. Especially in the driving last movement, it corresponds to what most people think of as 'Hungarian' music, although its folk-like melodies and rhythms are Bartók's own. Of great appeal is the short 'ritornello' or refrain that connects the movements and is treated differently each time it appears. The first statement is as follows:

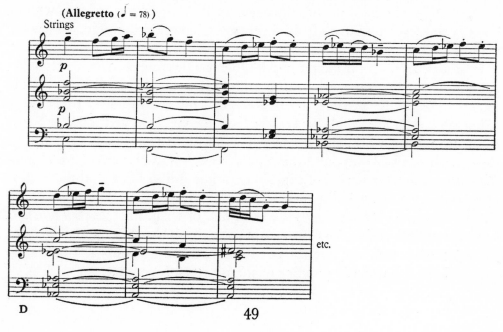

In 1923 Bartók married for the second time. Again he chose one of his pupils, sixteen-year-old Ditta Pasztory, a talented pianist with whom he gave occasional concerts towards the end of his life. The following year, Bartók's second son, Péter, was born; his first son, Béla jr., was fourteen at that time.

From now on, Bartók's life followed a fairly regular pattern: teaching at the Academy of Music; frequent concerts abroad; work on the huge mass of folk music he had collected before the First World War; and sporadic bursts of composition. A more opportunistic composer would have followed up the success of the Dance Suite with new pieces in the same vein. Instead, Bartók wrote very little music at first. And when he did begin to compose again, it was music of quite a different sort, much less likely to win friends easily.

A new period of creation begins in 1926 with his first and only Piano Sonata and the First Piano Concerto. Both are uncompromising, dissonant, aggressive pieces, which at that time frightened the average concert-goer out of his wits—and out of the concert hall. These were followed in 1927 and 1928 by the Third and Fourth String Quartets, which were even harder to understand and which seemed hopelessly 'modernistic' to audiences of those years. They are, as a matter of fact, the most 'radical' works Bartók ever wrote. During the late 1920s, he seems to have been experimenting with new techniques and idioms, just as many other composers were. On the one hand, there were the Neo-classicists, headed by Stravinsky; on the other, the atonalists and twelve-tone composers of the Schoenberg school, who no longer considered tonality a fruitful method of composition. Bartók followed neither of these prevailing directions but continued to write his own music, as he saw it. In the Third and Fourth Quartets he came as close to atonality as he was ever to come, without abandoning a tonal centre, however obscured it might be at times by dissonance and contrapuntal procedures.

Bartók hardly ever spoke or wrote about his views on aesthetics or about his own creative work. But his next compositions were more orthodox in their harmonic make-up, and this would seem to indicate that he had gone through a four-year period of experimentation and decided that for him, at least, tonality was an indispensable basis of composition. The magnificent *Twenty Hungarian Folksongs for Voice and Piano* of 1929, the *Cantata Profana* of 1930 and the Second Piano Concerto of 1931 are all based on tonal principles, extended to include the free use of dissonance and certainly not bound by the traditional harmonic practice of the nineteenth century.

CANTATA PROFANA

A kilenc csodaszarvas / Die Zauberhirsche

A facsimile of the first manuscript page of Bartók's *Cantata Profana* as it was
published in 1934.

VIII

The String Quartets

Because of their importance and central position in Bartók's work, the string quartets warrant our special attention. From the First Quartet of 1908 to the Sixth Quartet of 1939, they span most of Bartók's mature years as a composer and provide a concentrated summary, as it were, of his spiritual, musical and stylistic development.

The First Quartet looks towards the past and future at the same time. On the one hand, it is a 'romantic' work, especially in its chromatic harmony. We are reminded at times of Wagner, Brahms and Bruckner, but also, in some passages, of Debussy, whom Bartók had just discovered at that time. The main inspiration, however, is clearly the Beethoven of the late quartets. The first movement begins with a slow fugal section, recalling Beethoven's Quartet in C sharp minor, opus 131. Certain things in the second movement, especially the way the material is worked out in the development section, point in the same direction. And who can miss the resemblance between the fugue of the last movement and the *Grosse Fuge* of Beethoven? There is no question of a direct *influence* of Beethoven, whom Bartók admired above all other composers. But it is clear that Bartók has learned much from the Master of Bonn. He applies this knowledge, or, better still, this insight into the nature of music, in his own way. And he continues to do so to the end of his days.

The First Quartet also displays certain typically Bartókian traits that look towards his later works. First of all, there is the remarkable economy in utilizing the thematic material; the entire quartet can be analysed as an elaboration of the first movement. Then there is the leading role given to counterpoint, which will remain the basis of much of Bartók's subsequent writing. And finally there is the enormous rhythmic vitality of many passages.

All of these traits are present in the Second Quartet (1917), which is less 'romantic', but certainly no less expressive, than the first. There are few reminiscences of Brahms or Bruckner; traditional harmonic concepts no longer apply. Frequently one feels a tonal centre (created partly by pedal points), but in general the linear aspect is the most important, except in those passages where sheer driving rhythm takes over.

Ten years separate the Second from the Third Quartet (1927), which

From *String Quartet No. 6:* first movement

forms a pair with the Fourth Quartet (1928). These two works, with their sharp dissonances, involved contrapuntal textures and strange new instrumental sounds, are more 'objective' in style than any of the others. The music is highly expressive, but it is hard to say just *what* is being expressed. In both pieces, Bartók works constantly with short germ-motives which are varied, expanded and developed to produce ever-new material; there are few melodies or themes in the usual sense. The harmonies range from tonal to bi-tonal, poly-tonal and seemingly atonal, although the ear can always pick out instinctively a tonal centre, no matter how veiled it may sometimes be.

Like the Fourth Quartet, the Fifth (1934) is built in 'arch' form. The first and fifth movements share common thematic material, as do the second and fourth; the 'keystone' third movements have more or less independent material, although one can trace relationships even here. Stylistically, the Fifth presents fewer problems for the listener than the preceding two.

The Sixth Quartet (1939) is even more traditional in its harmonic idiom, and this fact has led some critics to accuse Bartók of progressing backwards. This criticism seems quite unjust. In the first place, modernity is no proper measure of quality. And besides, the Sixth is in many ways the crowning glory of Bartók's quartets and an apotheosis of all that has gone before. It is a work of complete maturity, in which idiom, and even technique, are of far less importance than the expression. It is hard to say just what the emotional content of this masterpiece is. More than any other it resembles the late Beethoven quartets in its universal expression, which is far removed from the more subjective expression of the earlier works. In the Sixth, and especially in its closing movement, Bartók reveals the tragedy of our century in a quiet language that combines deep tenderness with high nobility, but that does not hesitate to face the truth.

IX

America Visited

Between December 1927 and March 1928 Bartók made his first visit to America. Sponsored by the Pro Musica Society, he gave recitals in Chicago, St. Paul, Kansas City, Denver, Seattle, San Francisco and elsewhere, and he appeared with an orchestra in New York, Boston, Philadelphia and Cincinnati.

His début with the New York Philharmonic was of course the most important concert, and here he was plagued with his usual bad luck. The famous conductor Willem Mengelberg had programmed Bartók's new First Piano Concerto, but at the last minute he switched to the First Rhapsody for Piano and Orchestra, opus 1, from the year 1904. The American press had heralded Bartók as a wild, modernistic lion: the music was that of a very tame lamb. Quite justly the chief critic of the *New York Times*, Olin Downes, wrote that the work was 'interesting but immature and rather old-fashioned, comparatively ineffective, so free in style it lacks cohesion and concentration'. Downes criticized Mengelberg's inexact accompaniment and praised Bartók's 'born instinct for the keyboard, with poetry of conception and at times a fury of virtuosity and élan astonishing in a man of his modesty and unostentation'.

All in all, Bartók made only a slight impression during his American tour. His retiring manner was in sharp contrast with the kind of advance publicity he received, such as the headline: 'Hungarian Modernist Advances upon Los Angeles to Convince Scoffers.' Besides, Bartók's podium behaviour was most unspectacular. He indulged in no theatrical poses or gestures, and he sometimes played from music. Nevertheless, Bartók was pleased with the country and with its people. From Seattle he wrote to his mother: 'The people are everywhere very friendly; they take me on sight-seeing trips, they want to show me everything, and they are most unhappy when bad weather gets in the way. They are interested in everything and want to keep pace with the times, but they sometimes have trouble in doing so.'

America Visited

In the same year that he finished his American tour, 1928, Bartók received the good news that his Third String Quartet had won a prize in a competition sponsored by the Musical Fund Society of Philadelphia. The first prize of 6,000 dollars was divided, in fact, between Bartók and Alfredo Casella. In retrospect, the decision seems curious, for who would compare these two composers today? But one must give the jury credit; among 600 scores submitted, it singled out the one masterpiece. For Bartók, who never had more than enough for a modest living, the money was extremely welcome. And so, of course, was the recognition.

In January 1929, Bartók made his first and last tour of the Soviet Union, playing in Leningrad, Odessa, Kiev and other cities. Despite many complications caused by the Russian concert bureau's inefficiency he enjoyed the trip. In a letter to his wife he commented on the friendliness of the people and the enthusiasm of the audiences. The climate did not agree with him, however. He caught a bad cold and returned to Budapest completely exhausted and with a fever.

X

The Mature Master

On 25 March 1931, Béla Bartók celebrated his fiftieth birthday. Festivities were conspicuous by their absence. The world at large had not yet the slightest inkling that the quiet Hungarian 'modernist' was one of the great composers of this century. In Budapest, a performance of *The Miraculous Mandarin* had been planned, but it fell through when Bartók refused to make certain changes demanded by the local opera house.

In general, however, Bartók had some reason to be encouraged with the way things had gone during the past decade. He had achieved a certain amount of recognition, especially in professional circles, as a composer, pianist and folklore expert. Since 1923 he had had a close connection with one of Europe's leading publishers, Universal Edition. Despite recurring illnesses, his health was better than usual. And his physical wants were taken care of by his regular salary from the Academy of Music, supplemented by his concert appearances but diminished by the amounts he spent from his own pocket for his folk music work.

It is not likely, however, that Bartók was content with life. His was an unquiet spirit that knew neither peace of mind nor happiness in the usual sense. He was not very ambitious for worldly success. But he knew the value of his music, and it irritated him that his works were neglected. Even more, he was irritated by the injustice, treachery and stupidity that are part and parcel of civilization.

Bartók could never reconcile himself to city life, yet because of his profession he had to spend most of his life in cities. He always dreamed of the 'simple, wholesome' life of the peasants. Whether he would have kept his illusions if he had gone to live with the peasants is beside the point. What he did *not* know seemed to him far better than what he *did* know all too well.

At a time when he was most closely connected with cities and civilization, Bartók wrote his great hymn to Nature: *Cantata Profana*. He took the text from an old Rumanian folk ballad. The legend tells of nine brothers who are turned by magic into stags while they are hunting. When their father recognizes them and begs them to return home, they refuse, saying: 'We shall not go with you, for our antlers cannot go through doors, only through mountains . . . our mouths cannot drink from beakers, only from cool springs.' The symbolism is clear: the cool springs are the free world of nature; 'home' stands for the artificial world of civilization. One can also interpret the work as meaning the desire of man for freedom—personal or political, or both.

Bartók set this folk poetry for double mixed chorus, tenor and baritone soloists and orchestra. It is his largest choral work and one of the finest of the twentieth century. It is very difficult to perform, and this fact probably accounts for its comparative neglect. From the beginning, it has had bad luck. Composed in 1930, it was first performed four years later by the BBC Chorus and Orchestra. Perhaps the performance was at fault; in all events, the British press was not enthusiastic. The *Cantata Profana* remains, however, one of Bartók's most important works.

During the summer of 1931 Bartók attended a meeting in Geneva of the League of Nation's 'International Committee for Intellectual Cooperation', to which he was the Hungarian delegate. An individualist through and through, Bartók was fairly sceptical as to the usefulness of such political-cultural organizations, but he presented a project that had to do with recordings. As he wrote to his mother: 'the result will be nothing at all. The other resolutions will doubtless suffer the same fate. The major benefit is that these 20 or 25 people could meet each other and talk together.' Among the delegates who impressed Bartók the most was the German writer, Thomas Mann, with whom he held long conversations.

From Geneva he went to the Mondsee near Salzburg where he taught at a curious sort of summer school, the Austro-American Conservatory. Here an excellent faculty waited in vain for students to arrive. Bartók had three; some teachers had none at all. Bartók wrote to his mother that the whole thing 'turned out to be a monkey-comedy', but that he was paid well and promptly.

The year 1931 saw the birth of two major compositions: the magnificent Second Piano Concerto and the 44 Duos for Two Violins, in which Bartók makes free use of Hungarian, Serbian, Arabian, Slovakian, Ruthenian and Ukranian folksongs. Both works reflect his involvement with old music. He published arrangements of such composers as Domenico Scarlatti, Couperin, Zipoli, Rossi, Frescobaldi, Marcello and others as well as annotated editions

From *Music for Strings, Percussion and Celesta:* first movement

of Beethoven, Mozart, Haydn and Bach. In 1928, Bartók said in an interview published by the *Christian Science Monitor* that he had become more and more interested in pre-classical composers and that his own music was more contrapuntal than formerly. This shift in accent is extremely clear in the 44 Duos, which employ many contrapuntal devices, and the Second Piano Concerto often has a Bachian flavour, translated into Bartók's own language. Contrapuntal procedures are also prominent in his later works as well—in the canons of the Fifth String Quartet, the fugue of the *Music for Strings, Percussion and Celesta*. And in the complicated textures of the Sonata for Two Pianos and Percussion, the Third Piano Concerto, the Concerto for Orchestra and even in the Sonata for Solo Violin, counterpoint plays a leading role.

After a five-year burst of creativity, between 1926 and 1931, there followed a period of nearly three years during which Bartók wrote no major work. During this time, he gave many concerts abroad and worked at home on his book on Slovakian folksong. The story of this huge project is a long and sad one. It goes back to 1906, when Bartók began collecting Slovakian folk music, and continues to the end of his life. In 1921 he signed a contract for publication of the 2,600 folk melodies with a Slovakian publisher. After many delays, he threatened to withdraw the manuscript in 1932. Thereupon the publisher promised to bring out the work very soon, and Bartók spent much time and energy getting it ready for printing. But again nothing happened, and it was only in 1959, fourteen years after Bartók's death, that the first volume of *Slovakian Folksongs* appeared, published in Bratislava.

Concerts took Bartók to London and Paris in the winter of 1932. In April he attended a Folk Music Congress in Cairo. In January of 1933, he played his new Second Piano Concerto in Frankfurt, with Hans Rosbaud conducting, then at the I.S.C.M. Festival in Amsterdam. Here the work had such a success that Bartók was invited to perform it in London, Vienna, Zurich, Stockholm and several other cities. The first performance in Budapest was played by the Hungarian-born pianist Louis Kentner. For some time Bartók had refused to appear there in public because of the 'indifference and animosity of my own countrymen', as he wrote. 'Eighty or even ninety per cent of Hungary's educated society consider me a traitor because I study and propagate the music of the Hungarian villages (instead of the so-called "Hungarian melodies" that are really art music).'

For years Bartók was indeed a prophet without honour in his own country, ignored by all but a handful of admirers. His conservative compatriots could not follow his shockingly modernistic music. And he was openly attacked for his interest in non-Hungarian folk music. It was a time when Hungary was blindly supported by its people. Bartók found this disagreeable for, although he was patriotic towards his country, he had opinions of his own.

In 1934 a welcome change occurred in Bartók's life. He was commissioned by the Hungarian Ministry of Culture to spend the major part of his time working on the huge quantity of folk music that had accumulated in the Academy of Sciences. Now he no longer needed to teach piano at the Academy of Music and could devote himself almost exclusively to folk music research. This had long been his dream; that he was not able to complete the project was a bitter disappointment.

It is hard to say when Bartók would have started composing again if he had not been commissioned by the Elizabeth Sprague Coolidge Foundation in Washington to write a new quartet. The result was the Fifth, which was first performed by the Kolisch Quartet in April 1935. It was the beginning of a new creative period that produced some of Bartók's greatest works.

In early 1936, Bartók was made a member of the Hungarian Academy of Sciences, the first official honour he received in his own country. He had been made a Chevalier of the French Legion of Honour in 1930. In October of the same year he made his last folk music expedition. Invited by the Turkish government to lecture and give piano recitals in Ankara, he combined these activities with a trip to Anatolia. There in the desert he used his old Edison recording machine for the last time to record the music of the Mohammedan nomads.

It is amazing how one man could influence the course of music history. The Swiss conductor Paul Sacher was among the first to recognize the true stature of Béla Bartók. And Sacher was in the fortunate position of being able to do something about it. Thanks directly to him, Bartók wrote three masterpieces of the twentieth century: *Music for Strings, Percussion and Celesta, Sonata for Two Pianos and Percussion* and *Divertimento for String Orchestra*. These are Bartók's 'Basle' works, and they are among his best.

Bartók's friendship with Sacher goes back to 1929, when Bartók took part in a concert of his works given by the Basle section of the I.S.C.M. From then on, Sacher played Bartók's music frequently, and Bartók often went to Basle to visit him. When he played his Second Piano Concerto with Sacher's orchestra in 1935, it was clear to the Swiss conductor that Bartók was one of the great composers of that time. For the tenth anniversary of his *Baseler Kammerorchester* he commissioned the *Music for Strings*, which was given its première on 21st January 1937.

A detailed analysis of this composition would fill pages. It is a supreme example of Bartók's method of 'expanding' a germ motive or theme to supply the material for an entire work. This 'tight' construction gives the work a strong sense of unity and continuity. But the listener is not conscious of the construction, only of the profound meaning of the music—a meaning that is deeply felt but cannot be put into words.

During the summer of 1937, Bartók wrote his second Basle masterpiece: *Sonata for Two Pianos and Percussion*. At the première, in January 1938, he and his wife, Ditta, played the two piano parts. In a letter to his pupil, Wilhelmine Creel, Bartók wrote: 'It was a "mighty" success. Mrs. Bartók played very well—it was her first public appearance in a foreign country. After this première I had to travel, alone, to Luxembourg, Brussels, Amsterdam, The Hague and London . . . to earn some money.'

In style and expression, the Sonata for Two Pianos and the Music for Strings belong together. Both are intensely emotional in a restrained, almost impersonal way. Only occasionally does Bartók release driving, elemental rhythms. An air of mystery pervades many sections of the two pieces—especially in their slow, chromatic beginnings and in the strange sounds of the third movement in the Music for Strings—an example of Bartók's 'night music'.

Paul Sacher describes Bartók at rehearsals: 'Bartók's exactness was amazing. He always had a metronome with him to check the tempos, even when he played. He knew precisely what he wanted and demanded the ultimate in differentiated precision from everyone. Yet he was very patient, never offended . . . and truly modest.'

The Divertimento for String Orchestra was written in the incredibly short time of two weeks. The score is dated '2–17. August 1939'. Paul Sacher, who commissioned the piece, had invited Bartók to spend part of the summer in an idyllic chalet in Saanen, near Gstaad, and it was here that Bartók wrote the piece and worked on the Sixth String Quartet. The first performance of the Divertimento took place in July of 1940. Bartók could not be present, because he was putting his affairs in order before emigrating to America.

The title Divertimento is misleading, for this is a serious work that speaks of suffering but also of hope. Stylistically, it is quite different from the two other Basle compositions. It is far less difficult to understand, less complicated, more traditional in its idiom. Some critics have called Bartók's change to a more accessible style in his last works a 'compromise', aimed at making the music more successful. Anyone who knows Bartók's character at all must realize that he was incapable of compromise at *any* time of his life. The explanation is probably quite different. In his last works—the Divertimento, the Sixth Quartet and those he wrote in America—Bartók seems consciously to be speaking a more human, a more easily understood language in the hope that his message will reach a greater number of people. Like every great composer, Bartók knew perfectly well that style as such is of little importance, that it is the content, the message that matters. In all events, the assertion that Bartók 'changed styles' to please American taste is wrong. The change occurred in the two last works he composed in Europe.

Bartók was never a political man. After his brief chauvinistic 'seizure' of 1903–4, he took no active part in politics, and he seldom expressed a political opinion. He was, in the best sense of the word, a patriot, who loved his country, but never blindly, and who brought great honour to his country as an artist and as a human being.

From 1931 onwards, however, Bartók was forced to take note of political developments, which gradually were to change his life and drive him from his own land. In that year the great Italian conductor Arturo Toscanini left his native country in protest, after having refused to play the Fascist anthem *Giovanezza* before a concert. A Hungarian committee, headed by Bartók, drew up a resolution protesting against this scandalous affair.

In 1933 Adolf Hitler and the German National Socialist Party came to power and one of the blackest chapters in modern history began. Violently opposed to any system that suppresses individual freedom, Bartók became increasingly alarmed as Nazism spread and became more powerful. In a long series of letters to his friends, Professor and Mrs. Müller-Widmann in Basle, he mentions political matters more and more frequently. In the summer of 1937 he wrote: 'We had originally intended going to Italy (Dolomites), but recently my hate of Italy has become so abnormally great, that I simply cannot make myself set foot in it.'

The annexation of Austria by Nazi Germany was a great shock to Bartók. Moreover, it affected him directly. Again to Mrs. Müller-Widmann he wrote of 'the imminent danger that Hungary too will surrender to this system of robbers and murderers. . . . Not only has my publisher (Universal Edition) become a Nazi house (the owners and directors were simply thrown out) but they have also "Nazified" the Performing Rights Society to which I belong.'

The new Nazi management in Vienna sent Bartók a questionnaire, which he ignored. But in a moment of bitter humour, he wrote how he *might* have filled it out. To the question 'Are you of German blood, racially related or non-Aryan?' he would have answered 'Non-Aryan, because Aryan means Indo-European; we Hungarians are Finno-Ugrics, according to my lexicon.'

And to the question 'Where and when were you wounded?' the answer would have been 'On March 11, 12 and 13, in Vienna' (the days of the German occupation of Austria). Fortunately, the British firm of Boosey and Hawkes replaced Universal Edition as Bartók's publisher, and he soon became a member of the British Performing Right Society, known throughout the world as the P.R.S.

Bartók forebade the performance of his music in Germany—or in any radio station that could be heard in Germany or Italy. He also took steps to save the manuscripts of his works, sending them to the Müller-Widmanns in Basle. For many months he thought about leaving Hungary, but he could not make up his mind. On the one hand, he saw the hopelessness of the situation in Hungary 'where nearly all the "educated" Christian people subscribe to the Nazi system: I am really ashamed to belong to this class . . .' On the other hand: 'Even in the best of circumstances, earning my daily bread in some foreign land would cause me such enormous difficulties and spiritual pain . . . that I cannot think of it. And then I have my mother here; should I leave her in the last years of her life? No, I cannot do that!'

Bartók's mother died in December of 1939. His grief was great, for he had been very close to his mother throughout his life. But with her death, one of the main reasons for staying in Hungary had vanished. In the spring of

Bartók's comment on the outbreak of the Second World War: his illustration for the Christmas song 'An angel from heaven . . .'

Left, with his son Péter: *below*,
Bartók aged fifty-six

Bartók with his second wife, Ditta, in 1938

Bartók at the piano

1940, Bartók paid a two-month visit to the United States, playing a few concerts and discussing plans for settling in America. Then he returned to Budapest where he put his affairs in order and played a farewell recital. In his last European letter, Bartók wrote to Mrs. Müller-Widmann: 'Now with a sad heart we say our adieu to you and yours—for how long, perhaps forever, who knows! The parting is hard, infinitely hard. . . . Actually, this journey is a leap into the unknown from the insupportable known. Not least of all because of my poor health; I mean the periarthritis, which has still not healed. God knows how, and how long, I shall be able to work over there.'

XI

The American Years

On 29 October 1940, Béla Bartók and his wife landed in New York after a long and difficult journey. On 26 September 1945, Bartók died there.

No period in Bartók's life has been so misunderstood, and in some cases, so deliberately misinterpreted, as these American years, which constitute the sad end to a tragic life. In particular the Americans have been accused of letting a great composer disintegrate, so to speak, before their very eyes, of refusing him proper recognition, of allowing him practically to die of hunger.

This part of the Bartók legend has been so crassly simplified and even falsified—consciously or unconsciously—that it is high time to separate truth from invention, facts from fiction.

To begin with, let us have a look at Bartók's situation when he arrived in the United States. It was by no means the first time that he had been in America. As a concert pianist he had travelled the entire country from coast to coast. He knew, therefore, what to expect. He had chosen America of his own volition when he made the difficult decision to leave his native country.

In early October he and his wife had left Budapest, travelled through Yugoslavia, Italy, Switzerland, France and Spain and boarded their ship in Lisbon. Somewhere along the way all their luggage was lost. Coming on top of the journey through war-torn Europe, this naturally put Bartók into a state of nerves. Finally, however, the luggage was located in Spain and was sent on to New York.

During his first months in America Bartók was publicly honoured on three occasions. Shortly after their arrival, he and his wife performed the Sonata for Two Pianos and Percussion in Town Hall at the invitation of the 'New Friends of Music'. Three weeks later the couple gave an entire programme in the same hall.

And on 25 November Bartók was given an honorary doctorate by Columbia University, one of the largest and most important universities of the United States. In his citation the President of the university referred to Bartók as 'distinguished teacher and master; internationally recognized authority on folk music, creator through his compositions of a musical style

For Children: No. 41

universally acknowledged to be one of the great contributions to the twentieth-century literature of music; a truly outstanding artist who has brought high distinction to the spiritual life of his country'.

In contrast to many others who in that turbulent period came to America with no prospects whatsoever, Bartók had the guarantee of a certain basic financial security. During his earlier visit to the United States, Columbia University had offered him a position which left him complete freedom while providing a salary of 3,000 dollars a year—not a princely sum, to be sure, but at that time quite enough to live on modestly. Bartók refused another, much more highly paid offer because it involved the teaching of composition. This Bartók had always refused to do, because he felt that composition could not be taught—or that he at least could not teach composition.

For two years Bartók worked at Columbia University as Visiting Associate in Music. He was his own master, he could come and go as he pleased, and he was free to accept additional lecturing or concert invitations. The fact that he did his chosen work with enormous conscientiousness corresponds entirely to Bartók's nature. He never accepted money which he had not earned in the most literal sense, not through his talent, his prestige or his reputation. The idea of accepting a salary from Columbia University and doing only a minimum of work in return would have seemed to him immoral.

Besides, he was doing precisely the kind of work which he most loved and for which he had voluntarily given many years of his life. In a letter to his son, Béla jr., Bartók remarked: 'The purpose of my appointment is that I should study and transcribe that incomparable body of Yugoslavian folk music which is here at Columbia. This is the real reason why I came here. Nowhere else in the world is there such material, and this is precisely the material I was lacking in Europe.'

After such a good beginning things ought really to have gone well for Bartók in America. But they did not go well. From 1942 on, his situation became constantly more difficult. Gradually he himself lost courage and confidence in the future.

What happened to turn such a good beginning into such a tragic finale? The difficulties were of two kinds: external ones which affected Bartók but against which he could do nothing; and internal, purely personal difficulties against which, given his nature, he was equally helpless.

On 7 December 1941 the American Naval Base at Pearl Harbour was attacked. After a few days the United States were at war. Total war brought with it all kinds of problems which affected every person in the country. Soon there was an acute housing shortage, and the Bartóks had a hard time to find a suitable dwelling. Bartók also had a certain amount of trouble with his residence permit and other papers, although he had much less trouble than most immigrants, since Bartók's case was treated as an exception by the American government. Nevertheless, he worried a great deal about his status as a foreigner.

From the beginning of 1943 on, he also had financial worries. After two years, Columbia University was not able to renew his appointment, which had been temporary, and his only regular source of income ceased. It would have been an easy matter, if he had not refused to accept any presents, loans, or financial help of any sort. Many tried to help him, directly or indirectly. All kinds of subterfuges were attempted, but each time Bartók saw through the plan and refused what he considered charity. He would not even accept money from his son Péter, who sent home part of his pay in the American Navy. When Péter returned, his father gave him back every penny that he had sent.

The fact that he had very few performances contributed to Bartók's low spirits. So did the scant success of the concerts which he gave, either alone or together with his wife. It soon became clear that his hope of establishing a concert career in America could not be realised.

Besides such personal worries, Bartók was increasingly concerned with the future of Hungary, of Europe and of the world. In 1942 he wrote: 'The most terrible thing of all is that the future looks absolutely black, even if we win.' And somewhat later: 'There is no end in sight—and the destruction of Europe (both in terms of human lives and works of art) continues without pause and without mercy.'

If he had been in good health, Bartók could have borne all this private and public misfortune much better. But he was slowly dying. At the beginning of 1943 his condition suddenly became critical. He suffered a complete collapse and had to be taken to hospital. This was the beginning of the end, for the sickness from which he suffered was an incurable disease of the blood—leukemia. The doctors tried to hide the truth from him, but Bartók realized that his illness was extremely serious. In June of 1943 he wrote: 'there is no hope of recovery and it is out of the question to take anywhere a job'.

This collapse took place in Cambridge, Massachusetts, where Bartók had just begun a series of guest lectures at Harvard University. Because of the high medical and hospital costs, his situation would have been desperate if the American Society of Composers, Authors and Publishers (A.S.C.A.P.) had not stepped in. Although Bartók was not a member of this organization —he belonged to the British Performing Right Society—A.S.C.A.P. took over all expenses for doctors, examinations, medicines, hospitals and rest cures. After Bartók had been released from hospital, he and his wife went to Saranac Lake, in the mountainous regions of northern New York State, at A.S.C.A.P.'s expense. In the winter of 1943–4 Bartók was sent alone to Ashville, North Carolina, and again it was A.S.C.A.P. that paid the bills.

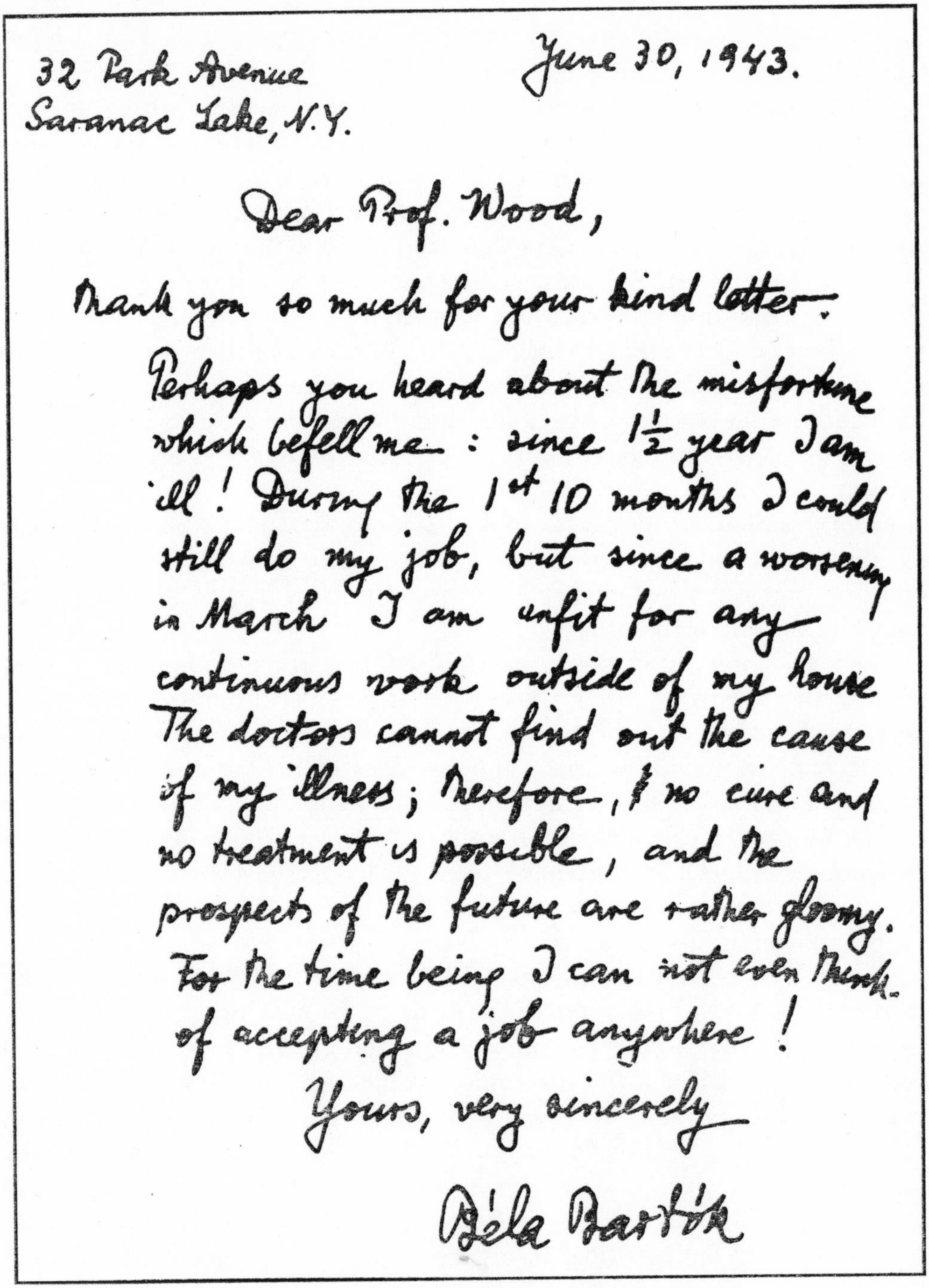

32 Park Avenue
Saranac Lake, N.Y.

June 30, 1943.

Dear Prof. Wood,

Thank you so much for your kind letter.

Perhaps you heard about the misfortune which befell me : since 1½ year I am ill! During the 1st 10 months I could still do my job, but since a worsening in March I am unfit for any continuous work outside of my house. The doctors cannot find out the cause of my illness; therefore, no cure and no treatment is possible, and the prospects of the future are rather gloomy. For the time being I can not even think of accepting a job anywhere!

Yours, very sincerely

Béla Bartók

A letter to Professor C. P. Wood from the composer, 1943

In the rural surroundings of Saranac Lake and Ashville, Bartók composed his last masterpieces—the Concerto for Orchestra, Sonata for Solo Violin, Third Piano Concerto, and the unfinished Viola Concerto.

The Concerto for Orchestra plays a very special part in Bartók's musical and personal fate. The circumstances of its composition recall those surrounding the *Requiem* of the dying Mozart. Mozart was approached by a mysterious stranger who in the name of a third person commissioned the *Requiem*. It was no unknown person who walked into Bartók's room in Doctor's Hospital but the great conductor Serge Koussevitsky, who asked Bartók to write an orchestral work in memory of his wife. This too, then, was to be a kind of requiem. He handed Bartók a cheque for half of the sum of the commission. Deeply moved, Bartók refused it: he was afraid that his health would not allow him to finish the work. But Koussevitsky begged Bartók to accept the commission. After some hesitation Bartók gave his consent.

From this moment his health took a sudden turn for the better. He soon left the hospital and went to Saranac Lake. There he worked almost night and day, and when in October he returned to New York City he brought with him the completed score.

The world premier of the Concerto for Orchestra took place in Boston on 1 December 1944; a few weeks later it was performed in New York, again by Koussevitsky and the Boston Symphony Orchestra. In both cities Bartók had triumphal successes, the last ones of his life and perhaps the greatest. This marked the beginning of Bartók's popularity, which has grown constantly ever since. Although the style of this work does not represent a compromise—Bartók would have been incapable of such a thing—it is nevertheless not so difficult as many of his other works. It is noble music, deeply moving in its humanity.

The interest aroused by this piece led to the performance of many other works by Bartók. Three years after his death he was the most frequently performed twentieth-century composer in the United States with the exception only of Richard Strauss and Prokofiev. But for Bartók himself recognition came too late. In Ashville he wrote the Sonata for Solo Violin, commissioned by Yehudi Menuhin. William Primrose commissioned the Viola Concerto, and Ralph Hawkes wanted to commission a new string quartet. Ethel Bartlett and Ray Robertson asked him to write a concerto for two pianos. For the first time in his life Bartók might have lived for years exclusively from commissions.

In 1945 Bartók's strength was exhausted. The creeping sickness returned more and more frequently. He had hoped to spend the summer with the Menuhins in California, but he had to cancel these plans. Instead he went again to Saranac Lake where in the mountain air he gathered his last energies to work on the Viola Concerto and the Third Piano Concerto. Then he returned to his little apartment in New York. On 22 September 1945 he was taken to West Side Hospital. Four days later he died.

Bartók's American years were solitary, sad years, full of disappointments. But would they have been any less sad, any less disappointing, any less solitary in any other country?

XII

Bartók the Man

éla Bartók was a strange and difficult man. He was also a great man and a great composer, one of the greatest of the twentieth century. To really understand his music, and to understand why he composed as he did, it is important to know what kind of a man he was, how he thought and how he reacted to the world around him.

As a man and as an artist, Bartók changed as he grew older. But he changed less than most people do; the essential qualities of his character and personality remained quite constant. A perceptive painter who might have painted Bartók's portrait in early manhood and again in his late years would have brought out the same traits in both portraits—as do the photographs of Bartók.

Perhaps his salient quality was his integrity—both as a person and as an artist. Again, one senses this in the photographs from all periods of his life. It is expressed in the clarity and intensity of his eyes. People who knew Bartók agree unanimously that his piercing glance saw everything and saw through everything. He would accept no humbug, and nobody was able to fool him. Nothing irritated him so much as pretence and cant.

Bartók's eyes mirrored his own integrity, which one associate of his described as being too angelic for this world. Bartók set himself the very highest standards of conduct and artistry, and he applied these standards to others as well. In a sense, this was unrealistic, for we all know that the world is not made up exclusively of angels, and even the best people have their weak moments. Bartók had a few such moments, but they were extremely rare.

The standards of perfection which Bartók applied to himself and expected of others often led to his being disappointed and offended. In a world in which compromises are made every day, Bartók refused to compromise, even when it would have been much to his advantage to do so. Throughout his life he remained an idealist, but by no means a starry-eyed one·

74

Bartók the Man

He had his eyes wide open; he knew that things and people were not as he wished them to be, but he continued to act and to judge as if they were. He could be called an 'idealistic realist' or a 'realistic idealist'. This is only one of the seeming contradictions in Bartók's complicated nature.

Bartók could never make his peace with the world as it is, the world in which one hand washes the other, in which deals are made and in which the struggle to progress often leads to ignoble behaviour. To protect himself against the everyday world which caused him pain, Bartók built a barrier of resistance round himself. He spoke very little, and hardly ever said anything

An American caricature of Bartók at the piano

about himself, his music or other subjects that touched him deeply. He gave the impression of being diffident and even uninterested. Only his few close friends knew the generous, more open side of his character. He had the reputation of being unapproachable, because he would not, or could not, engage in polite conversation and 'small talk'. He was totally unable to flatter; his silence meant approval, and a phrase like 'very good indeed' represented the highest praise in his vocabulary.

He never tried to sell himself or his works, but took the position that his music was good enough to make its own way. He knew the worth of his own music, and he expected others to see this, too. It would be quite wrong, however, to imagine that Bartók was indifferent to performances and to recognition. He was simply too proud to 'promote' his works or draw attention to himself. Nevertheless, it made him unhappy that his music was neglected, as it certainly was during his lifetime.

Béla Bartók was a solitary man. He had few close friends, and his acquaintances were on a fairly superficial plane. He was too tight-lipped to be a good mixer at parties, which he disliked in any event. Ninety per cent of his life he devoted to work and it was this that gave him the greatest pleasure. It was the kind of work he chose for himself and it is amazing how much this one person accomplished in his relatively short lifetime.

Bartók rarely said anything about his own music, and the occasional programme notes he wrote deal with purely formal, external matter. Composition was a sacred sphere, to which no other living mortal was allowed access. He refused to teach composition, for he felt that composition could not be taught, or at least that *he* could not teach it.

Bartók's relation to nature was very close and personal. He was happiest when he could leave cities and civilization behind him and spend some time in the country.

Suggestions for Further Reading

By far the best all-round book in any language is Halsey Stevens's *The Life and Music of Béla Bartók* (Oxford University Press). Other than this, there is no full-length book that can be recommended. Agatha Fassett's *The Naked Face of Genius* (Houghton Mifflin Company, Boston) purports to be a description of Bartók's American years but is a highly romanticized and unreliable work, containing some truth and a great deal of fantasy. An iconography, *Béla Bartók's Life in Pictures* (Boosey & Hawkes Limited) contains many interesting photos. For a more detailed study of Bartók's music, see the present author's chapter in *European Music in the Twentieth Century*, edited by Howard Hartog (Routledge & Kegan Paul). Bartók's letters have hitherto been available only in Hungarian, German and French. The publication of *Béla Bartók Letters* by Faber and Faber (1971) is extremely welcome, since it will give English-speaking readers access to these fascinating and important documents.

Short Summary of Bartók's Works

First String Quartet, 1909
Bluebeard's Castle, Opera in one act, 1911
The Wooden Prince, Ballet in one act, 1916
Second String Quartet, 1917
The Miraculous Mandarin, Pantomime in one act, 1919
Dance Suite, 1923

Mikrokosmos, 153 progressive pieces for piano, 1926–39
First Piano Concerto, 1926
Third String Quartet, 1929
Fourth String Quartet, 1928
Cantata Profana, 1930
Second Piano Concerto, 1931
Fifth String Quartet, 1934
Music for String Instruments, Percussion and Celesta, 1936
Sonata for Two Pianos and Percussion, 1937
Concerto for Violin and Orchestra, 1938
Divertimento for String Orchestra, 1939
Sixth String Quartet, 1939
Concerto for Orchestra, 1943
Third Piano Concerto, 1945

Index

Index